ARE WE THE FIVE AGGREGATES?

Understanding the Five Aggregates,
Their Characteristics and Their Workings

ARE WE THE FIVE AGGREGATES?

Understanding the Five Aggregates,
Their Characteristics and Their Workings

Commentary by

ZEN MASTER THÍCH TUỆ HẢI

English translation by Milam Sudhana
Edited by Oliver K. Luu

EKAYANA ZEN PUBLICATIONS

ISBN 9798861718189

First edition published by Ekayana Zen Publications, Irvine, California, USA.
Contact: *ekayanazen@gmail.com*
For digital information, please visit: *www.ekayanazen.com*

Printed in the United States of America

Book desgin: Pristine Nguyên

CONTENTS

$\mathcal{B}$reathing in
perfect *merit* and *wisdom*

$\mathcal{B}$reathing out
full of *love*

The following commentary is excerpted from a series of teaching of Zen Master Thich Tuệ Hải on the Essence of Prajñāpāramita during the Tranquil Dwelling Season at Long Hương Temple in 2019.

In the *Essence of Prajñāpāramita* (commonly known as the *Heart Sūtra*), the Buddha was talking about someone who has *transcended all five aggregates*. What then are the five aggregates or five heaps? If we speak of them in a most unpolished way to make them easiest to understand, the five aggregates are our body and mind.

Form, the aggregate of form, is our body form, and sensation, perception, mental formation (*karmic* formation), and consciousness are our mind. Anyone who directly experiences and directly sees the *"five aggregates as being Void"* means they are in a *noumenal* state where their bodies as vivid yet completely Void at the same time. Intrinsically, the five aggregates are *Prajñā in the vivid presence, pure Suchness* and *immaculate*. It is due to the nature of emptiness that everything can come into existence, yet, in actuality, it lacks a solid independent self.

If we still see that there is a body, then it means that we do not yet have the *Perfect Wisdom* and we have not yet transcended grasping, clinging and suffering. The *Naturally Free and Unobstructed Seeing One,* on the other hand, directly penetrates his physical body of four elements (earth, water, wind and fire) as being Void. Void does *not* mean that there is *"nothing"* in contrast to a substantial, solid form, but herein, Void points to the absolute empty-tranquil-immaculate state of being. This Void is neither the *"sign of form"* (existence) nor the *"sign of emptiness"* (non-existence). In other words, this is *"the Void of our innate nature."* Because this nature is innately Void, thus, from this very state of Voidness, Singless Void or Signlessness, there is *neither form nor formlessness,* it can give birth to *both existence and non-existence* at the very same time!

Therefore, the Awakened Being, herein, had a direct knowing with lucid clarity that his body and mind is, indeed, *Prajñā in the pristine presence.* This presence is Void and this presence is *Suchness.* That is the direct realization of a person whom we can say has *"immersed in" Prajñā.* Only those who would have enough wisdom can penetratively fathom the five aggregates, that which is their body and mind, as Void.

That is, at the very precise mental momentness, the Awakened Being came upon *Prajñā* in order to totally dissolve which he *"thoroughly penetrated"* all five aggregates as Void. I must say that hereby, it is not *"to observe through contemplative insight,"* as usually expressed in the classic translation of the Heart Sūtra, but rather, precisely at the momentness of pristine presence when this *Perfect All-Transcendent Wisdom* manifests, *that presence itself is,* indeed, *Prajñā!* Here, it is no longer a cognitive understanding and no longer the conscious mind's all-knowing, but rather the *direct, lucid and penetrating all-pervasive totality true knowing.*

If we clearly, penetratingly fathom *Prajñā,* then we can see that since time immemorial until now, there has *never* been any clinging or retention in the five aggregates. We mistakenly perceive everything so we have form, sensation, perception, mental formation and consciousness, yet when we finally see the truth as it is, then the five aggregates are innately, thoroughly unobstructed and themselves are the vivid presence. This brightly clear penetration does not mean that we are changing or altering our seeing and our view, but it simply means that since the past until now, our five aggregates inherently have always been Void.

Thus, when *Prajñā* vividly emerges then its lucid clarity will reveal the true existence of the five aggregates. The five aggregates have never had any substantial existence. When there is confusion, there are the five heaps; when there is direct knowing and direct penetration, then the five heaps are Void. This has nothing to do with *"to observe through contemplative insight"* nor *"to deeply course in,"* because all of those expressions are superfluous and lack the efficacy to express about *Prajñā*.

Furthermore, when we talk about *Prajñā*, the core essence of perfect wisdom, we are hereby talking about the *unobstructed penetration of the whole sphere of phenomenal truth*, the *dharmadātu* that inherently is Voidness – *a state of clear and dynamic manifestations yet signless, devoid of any characteristic signs*. This *dharmadhātu* is nonetheless the pristine presence, the realm of *True Suchness* devoid of any dissimilarity! That is the true equanimous, non-discriminatory state. So if we still see dissimilarities in that expanse of *Suchness*, then we do not possess the *Prajñā* wisdom.

This *Prajñā* itself clearly sees the intrinsic perfect truth of the five aggregates and the phenomena in the state of Voidness. It is *not* that now we have to *"engage in practicing exertion"* that the five aggregates become Void! Similarly, neither did the five aggregates always exist substantially, and then due to our practicing for a few dozen years, or for ten-thousand lives that finally, the five aggregates now *become* Void. It is not at all like that!

We are hereby talking about an Awakened Being, someone who has acquired the enlightened wisdom *completely without effort*. Thus, he can *"penetratingly fathom"* the five aggregates. This does *not* come from *"practicing exertion"* (Viet. *công phu*), nor due to his *"observance through contemplative insight"* (Viet.

quán chiếu), or through his *"practicing in the deep course"* (Viet. *hành thâm*). All of those classical terminologies are far-off from what is happening right now in this precise moment! Therefore, we need to set aside these old ideas in order to become receptive to *Prajñā* in this very vivid presence. If there is still anything of old that we are clinging to, then *Prajñā* cannot manifest in the presence.

Therefore, when an Awakened One finally attains complete enlightenment, nothing can be caught or retained in this state of pure, unadulterated beingness, and there is no chance for any residue of bondage or fear to possibly remain; he or she is freely, utterly liberated, where there is no coming, no going, no form, sensation, perception, mental formation and consciousness. On the other hand, if right now we see that there is still body and mind, and all sorts of other things, then it means that we are still trapped in the five aggregates.

When we study the Dharma and especially the *Essence of Prajñāpāramita*, we need to clearly understand the five aggregates – the components of our body and mind (*form, sensation, perception, mental formation and mental consciousness*), because if we do not completely see, understand, discern, and comprehend them correctly, we would be totally confused in our practice.

The aggregate of form

What is the "aggregate of form"? It is our physical body that consists of the four elements: earth, water, air and fire. *"Earth"* is anything that is hard which we can touch, such as head hair, body hair, teeth, nails, skin, flesh, tendon, bone, marrow, diaphragm, etc. *"Water"* is wet; anything that is wet is water, such as sweat, blood, pus, urine, etc. *"Air"* is movement. If our blood is still circulating, our circulatory system is still flowing, and if we can still breathe in and out, are in motion, stay alive, or have any movements, it is because there is air. *"Fire"* is body warmth. Any living creature in this universe without fail must have all of those four elements, and no one can possibly evade them.

How did the Buddha explain about the aggregate of form in the *Śūraṅgama Sūtra*? For example, in the middle of space, if we flick a lighter, then the lighter will spark, and if we flick a gas burner, then the burner will spark. Thus, fire exists everywhere in open space; however, it depends on our mind and what specific kind of fire we want to see. If we want to have enough fire for a pot of rice to be well cooked, then there would be enough fire on the burner to cook that rice, but if we want to have enough fire to burn down a house, then a fire will blaze to burn it down. Therefore, the fire corresponds with our mind. Thus, in light of this, the Buddha taught in the *Śūraṅgama Sūtra* that the four elements are *"the Tathāgatagarbha pervading the whole dharmadhātu, emanating in equipollence with the mag-*

nitude of the beings' understanding, being revealed according to the beings' karma."

In Buddhism, *Tathāgatagarbha* refers to the fully awakened matrix and essence, the eternal and immutable matrix of all reality, and the womb of the absolute. In short, it is the very core the essence of Buddhahood, the ultimate all-transcendental state.

An awakened being, therefore, can clearly, directly, and lucidly see the five aggregates as the *Tathāgatagarbha* and the four elements of nature (earth, water, air and fire) as the *Tathāgatagarbha*. In the very beginning, the perfect wisdom speaks of the peerless realm of an all-transcendental person who has gone beyond the cycle of birth and death, beyond all mundane knowledge and all past and present misconceptions in order to have a direct knowing of this form as the empty, transparent pristine presence without a single trace of clinging.

The reason we have not yet reached this realization is that we still see that our physical bodies still exist, that they are substantial, and that there is birth and death. However, according to an enlightened being, this bodily form has no arising (no birth) and no ceasing (no death). An enlightened being has a direct knowing that there is no gap or division between the outer four elements in the cosmos and the four elements inside our bodies. Just like in the Four Foundations of Mindfulness practice, when we meditate, we have to contemplate on the inner body and the outer body, and we will come upon the truth that the wetness on the outside does not have any rift with the wetness inside our bodies. Therefore, the earth, water, air and fire elements of our bodies, and the earth, water, air and fire elements of this universe are inherently the *Tathāgatagarbha, perfectly pure, ubiquitously pervading the whole dharmadātu,* with nothing being defiled.

11

In the view of an awakened being when the perfect wisdom emerges in the vivid presence, he or she directly penetrates the reality of the five aggregates, as well as the four elements of the body, as intrinsically immaculate, tranquil and empty, and arisen from the state of Voidness. Therefore, the appearance of the five aggregates is a false appearance formulated by our mental consciousness. Our mental consciousness is an illusion as well, and it constructs the illusive body whereas in reality, this illusive body does not exist.

Once one has a direct knowing of this truth, one will realize that all *dharmas* – all phenomena ever since the past until now – are inherently unborn, unceasing; there has never been birth and death. However, we are still being deluded, so in the view of mundane people like us, we have bodies, old age, sickness and death, and there is life-and-death without fail. However, this is a confused and deluded view, a view of ignorance. Even if, for an instant, we see that there is *"existence"* versus *"non-existence,"* then we have already fallen deep into the domain of ignorance. However, if we want to speak the language of *Prajñā,* we need to see that our body of four elements is intrinsically pure, and it is none other than the *Tathāgatagarbha,* pervading the whole sphere of phenomenal truth.

The aggregate of sensation

We usually understand the aggregate of sensation as containing the sensations of pleasantness, unpleasantness or neutrality. For example, we are sitting here listening to the teaching, having no feeling of unpleasantness, but not feeling too excited about it either, so that is a kind of neutral sensation. When we listen, if we do not really understand anything and we do not really like it either, then we are experiencing a sensation of neutrality. However, suddenly, when someone curses us, saying "you are just like a beast," then a sensation of irritation arises, and that is the sensation of unpleasantness. On the other hand, when someone praises us, telling us "how pretty you are, much younger than before," then we feel happy, and that is the sensation of pleasantness. Thus, we need to carefully examine from where happiness (pleasantness) and suffering (unpleasantness) arise.

The literal meaning of the term depicting *"sensation"* in Vietnamese is to receive, and this is the receiving aspect of the six-sense faculties or six-sense bases: eyes, ears, noses, tongue, body and mind. In order to receive, there must exist a consciousness which discerns, and through the working of this consciousness, sensation can be considered as our conviction and cognition. Whatever we receive is considered our sensation. For example, if someone wants to give us one hundred thousand dollars, and we accept it, then we are saying that we receive a favor from this person. Or we receive either a praise or an insulting word, a good thing, a bad thing, a circumstantial condition, a sound or a form. It is all considered receiving.

So when the six-sense faculties encounter the six-sense objects, that is receiving. We receive sensations all the time, from the outside all the way to the inside. When we have thoughts about the past, we might feel sad about a certain event because there was nothing pleasant about it. Yet, when we remember a happy pastime, we smile a little. When we feel sad, loved, angry or hatred, it means that we are receiving these sensations. Then, there are things in the past that just float by in our mind, and we feel rather normal about them as no sensation of suffering or happiness arises. Or there are things that are passing by, and we have no feeling about them; however, it is still a sensation.

When the sense faculties come into contact with the sense objects, then precisely at the moment when the contact happens, sensation appears. It is just like how it is explained in the twelve links of dependent origination: (1) *ignorance* links to *mental formation*, (2) *mental formation* links to *consciousness*, (3) *consciousness* links to *name-and-form*, (4) *name-and-form* links to the *six-sense bases*, (5) the *six-sense bases* links to *contact*, and (6) *contact* links to *sensation*. Thus, no matter what contact happens between the sense faculties and sense objects, all of that is considered sensation. Sensation, again, is receiving, and the way we Vietnamese usually denote it is called *"lãnh đủ"* or *"to take it all."* When someone curses us with just one word, or strikes us with just one strike, we *"bear it all."* For almost all of our life, there has not been a time when we do not have sensation or do not receive the sensation.

The feeling or the sensation of this body is contact. When we come into contact with the heat, it is a sensation of heat; with the cold, a sensation of coldness; with smoothness, a sensation of smoothness; with roughness, a sensation of roughness; with pain, a sensation of pain. Just like when a needle first touches our skin, there is no feeling yet, but when it prickles hard, then there is pain, then there appears the feeling, the sensation of the body. Therefore, sensation is not just of the mind, but also of the body. Both body and mind have sensation, including those of the eyes, ears, nose, tongue and body. It does not mean sensation only involves the mind, like what we have studied all this time that sensation is the mind. If that is the case, then we have not yet fully learned about sensation.

When there is sensation, there is (8) *craving (or desire).*[1] Craving does not only mean loving affection, but it is both love and hate. Hate is a form of craving, but it is in opposition to love. When we have craving, we have (9) *grasping (attachment* or *possession);* when we love, we crave; when we hate, we also crave. When we love, we give rise to a thought, and when we hate, a thought also arises in our mind; therefore, when love and hate are combined, it becomes grasping. When we hate, we keep it in our heart-mind, and when we do not hate, we also keep it. When there is love, there is grasping, but when there is hate, there is even deeper grasping. The two things that are the most difficult to forget are love and hate. The name for both love and hate, is craving. Craving is not just love and fondness, as when there is hate, you have even deeper grasping. There is a saying in Vietnamese about hate: "When we are alive, we keep it in our heart; when we die, we bring it with us." It means our senti-ments are so thick that our remembrance of it becomes so persistent. That is the other side of craving. Thus, craving has two sides, love and hate. Grasping is borne from craving.

---

[1] In English, the eighth link is expressed as *"craving"* whereas in Vietnamese, it is termed as *"ái"* which denotes *"desirous love."*

Even though there is no affection, no hatred, no suffering, no happiness, there is still receiving. Just like when we look at this table, we do not hate it or have any affection toward it, but we do receive it. When our eyes encounter a form, we already receive it. It has become a habitual tendency of grasping or clinging of the sense faculties toward the sense objects. As we see, we immediately receive it. As we hear, we immediately receive it, and we cannot possible reject it. However, for an enlightened being, right at the moment they see something, they do not receive it or accept it; thus, it is called without sensation. They do not even have any neutral sensation where there is no sensation of pleasantness or unpleasantness. For us, there is still the neutral sensation; we cannot elude the neutral sensation.

For example, although we did not have any feeling for a specific person, the moment we saw them, we already received them. Why aren't there any sentiments though? Because there were no sad, loving, angry or hateful memories between this person and us; we just saw them for the sake of seeing. However, after we came home, did we think of them? Yes, we remembered about them, although we felt no love or hatred toward them. Therefore, that, too, is sensation. Without sensation, would we remember them? No. Nevertheless, there are things that we remember about which bring no suffering or happiness to us. For example, like how we ate our meal yesterday, and how it was very simple and normal. Or when we put our feet down on the ground, and how it was such a normal thing to do; there was no pleasantness or unpleasantness, yet there was a sensation. Or when our bottom touches the chair, that is sensation. The wind blows and touches our bodies; that, too, is sensation. Although it is not colored by pleasantness or unpleasantness, our own bodies and mind still have the sensation.

The aggregate of perception

In the *Sūtra*, *"perception"* is called *"cognition"* (Viet. *tri*), but this is not the *totality all-encompassing all-pervasive knowing* capacity. When we sit back, all of the mental impressions of the sense objects which we previously encountered, such as when our eyes see, our ears hear, our nose smells, our tongue tastes, and our body touches, would still fill our heads. The Mind Only School refers to them as the *"mental imageries imputed from form appearances"* or the *"purely imaginary, imputative mental impressions"* (Viet. *lạc tạ ảnh tử* or *tịnh sắc căn*). These mental impressions are conceptual imageries that still remain in our consciousness because our sense faculties had at one time come into contact with the sense objects. If we have never encounter-ed something, can we now have perceptions of that? Can we have perception of something that we have never heard, seen, understood or come to know? Can we at all perceive what it is like, that which we have never come into contact? For example, when we say that the beings in the God Realm are gorgeous looking, then how can we perceive or imagine that kind of beauty? We really cannot imagine nor have perception about their gorgeousness if our sense faculties have never met the sense objects. That is the first type of perception

There is also another way that we can imagine using our prior conceptual knowledge. For example, we had a very deep cut on our hand at one time which took a month to heal. Now we just had another cut, and we imagined that this cut would take another month to heal, but this time it turned out to be just a mild cut, and so it was healed after a few days. Or when we were wading in the rice fields and there were some leeches latching on to us. In the beginning when we did not notice them, they seemed like nothing, but if the person next to us started to say, "Oh, look, leeches are latching on you, how disgusting!" and after that we would drop unconscious. Because when there is any kind of perception involved, things usually multiply or expand. For example, there was a child who was playing and accidentally caused a bird to die, and there was this lady who happened to see it. She would go home to tell everyone that this morning, she saw a boy who beat up an eagle to death. People imagine and make small things big. We, too, are always like that. We rely on old stories, and use our imagination to blow them out of proportion to make them bigger than what they really are.

When we are sitting by ourselves, all these good, bad, wonderful, terrible, old and new stories would appear, and these are called thoughts or mental imageries. We should also mention something about our practice so that we can better understand what takes place here. When a mental impression or thought arises and we can clearly see it when it arises, then that very thought would automatically dissolve. We, however, would rather not let them self-appear and then self-disappear. Instead, we want to *"practice,"* which means when thoughts appear, we want to eliminate them. Nevertheless, wanting to eliminate them is actually to think of them even more deeply, and they will certainly come back to us! It is because we ourselves want to give water and manure to these mental impressions, and we already begin to want to retain them in this way. The very attitude of wanting to remove or to eliminate thoughts during meditation practice is in itself an erroneous mindset. Wanting to reject, to remove, to be separated from a delusional thought, or wanting it to stop existing or to be terminated... all of those wants or desires are simply mistakes!

Thus, when thoughts happen, when past stories vaguely return, they appear right in front of us. Then *"they"* remember this and remember that, *"they"* love this person or hate that person, then we just leave *"them"* alone and let *"them"* take their own normal course, and we can just simply be the seers who are clearly aware of everything. When our *"knowing-awareness in the vivid presence"* manifests, we clearly recognize whatever appears, but we do not label it as delusion, attachment, hate or ignorance, and we do not need to compete with it, oppose, criticize or disparage it. All thoughts will be *"clearly seen, clearly known"* and they self-dissolve. Slowly, thoughts of the past will become sparse, because when thoughts arrive, we do not give them any importance. When there are guests coming to our house, if we do not receive and entertain them, not offering them any tea or water, they will be bored, and then they will not come again. Similarly, thoughts will slowly become sparse.

It is this naturally transparent *"knowing-awareness in the vivid presence"* that gets clearer and more lucid over time. In the beginning, we would clearly recognize coarse thoughts, and then, subtle thoughts, and then thoughts slowly and ever so slowly become sparse, and then there are no more thoughts for us to recognize. By then, we would lucidly know that it is empty-hollow, and by then, the aggregate of perception is considered extinct.

In the beginning, the mental imageries, sounds, and the coming together of sense faculties and sense objects give rise to perception. If we have not been exposed to the sense objects, we cannot possibly perceive them nor remember them. There-fore, thoughts arise because we have previously encountered the objects. Thoughts are deluded movements and delusional arisings, and they are the causal seeds of birth and death. If the aggregate of perception becomes extinct, would that end birth and death? No! If we are looking at it from a shallow, narrow-minded perspective, we think that when all illusive thoughts come to a complete rest, then there is no more birth and death. However, in actuality, it still has not ended!

When we are sitting still to calm down all of our thoughts, then a state of *"thoughtless"* or *"non-thought"* and non-perceptional tranquility will appear in our mind. There will be no more thoughts, no more elaborated ideas, and no more hustle and confusion. That is when we are considered to have meditative absorption. In the beginning, this concentration is void and tranquil, but when our absorption gets much deeper, we would see the surging, flooding torrent of mental arisings of the aggregate of mental formation. These arisings are no longer discursive thoughts like those of the aggregate of perception.

Perception, therefore, is like bubbles floating on the surface of the sea, but mental formation is the entire vast ocean. The causal seeds of birth and death, however, do not lie on the outer surface of the aggregate of perception but in the aggregate of mental formation. It turns out that the aggregate of mental formation is the covert lair of *samsara,* the cycle of life-and-death. In reality, not too many people have enough meditation competence or wisdom capability to be able to see the aggregate of mental formation. Only those who transcend the aggregate of perception can actually encounter mental formation.

The *Śūraṅgama Sūtra* says that *"emotions (afflictions) will bring you down, and perception can lead you up."* However, we can only go upward if we *no longer have* perception! If we still have perception, then we must be very careful, because we may still end up in any realm, including the hell realm.

It is the same with us sitting here. If our perception has settled, then automatically our body and mind feel light. Therefore, sometimes people sit in meditation and feel their bodies are gently floating, and they are not wrong about that, because when perception has settled down, then spontaneously, the physical body is no longer real.

When we see that there is a substantially real body, that is because we are seeing with perception. When perception has diminished, even if we weigh 100 kilograms, we still feel that we do not carry any density, and our bodies would feel like a bag of cotton gliding on the ground. Therefore, as long as we still have emotions and perception, we will still feel heavy and go downward. Again, the *Śūraṅgama Sūtra* says that *"emotions will bring you down, perception can lead you up."* When I gave teachings in the past, I used to have some doubts about this. Today, however, I must affirm that emotions, as well as perception, will bring us down. With perception still intact, there is no way for us to rise above, because as long as there is perception, there will still be heaviness in body and in mind.

If we are bounded by anything, then we will still be weighed down. For example, if we are bounded by sensation then we will continue to give rise to perception. If we are bounded by perception, then we will still have this body. For a person whose perception has diminished, he or she will fall into a state of being *nearly* without body, but will not completely be without it yet. Only when we exert further in our practice to have the capability to transcend the aggregates of form, sensation and perception, then at that moment, we would completely come to be without our physical bodies. It is clear that if we can complete all three steps of transcending the aggregates of form, sensation and perception, then we would fall into a very deep state of meditative absorption. However, if you sit simply to

21

quiet down your mind then your absorption would not be too deep. These two states of meditative absorption are very different.

If we have already dismantled the aggregate of form through our meditation exertion, the sensations of the body will disappear. Feelings and sensitivities will disappear, and along with their disappearances, the aggregate of perception will become settled. If these trios (form, sensation, perception) altogether disintegrate leading to the experience of void, then our body and mind will dissolve completely and we will be in a very profound state of meditative absorption. There are people who reach this state and end up with supernatural powers. However, these practitioners still cannot conquer the cycle of birth and death, even though they have erroneously believed that they already attained *Arhatship* or sainthood at this stage.

As far as Buddhism is concerned, the Buddha knew that some-one can sit still, enter meditation absorption for one hundred years and dismantle his perception, and that all of his activities of body and mind would completely settle. However, that is not the place for the fruit of *Arhatship* or sainthood. *Arhatship* must take place where the aggregate of perception, mental formation and consciousness altogether extinguish. Perception is some-thing that gives us heaviness, and makes us see either existence or non-existence in this life. When there is still perception, everything becomes either existence and non-existence without fail. We have never been able to escape this duality, and the very first thing for us is to perceive that our body *"exists."* However, when perception comes to an end, we will utterly come to be *non-physical*. We would have a directly knowing that our body has no more weight and there is *no more mind*! When both body and mind are no more, it means that the *trio of form, sensation, and perception* would dissolve altogether, and thus,

22

we would fall into the mental state of being without body and mind, because perception has already become void.

When we are able to perceive, see and be aware of thoughts as they appear, this is at the level where we can just simply recognize, but perception is not the superlative state. When we still have many thoughts, then we need to be aware that we still have many thoughts. When thoughts are less, we know that we have fewer thoughts. When there are no more thoughts, then we can still see the transparent and tranquil void where there is no thought. This *"seer"* is not the same as the perception itself, and only then, can he clearly see and penetrate perception. This *"seer"* has enough capacity to see beyond perception and reach mental formation. The *"seer"* or the one who is seeing, in this case, is no longer perception. Only then can he have the ability to penetrate deeply into mental formation.

When we have too much perception, it causes our level of awareness to be less heightened, less subtle, and thus, we would not be able to penetrate all the way to the vast depths of the ocean of mental formation! We have not yet been able to see this. It is because we have not yet gone beyond perception, and therefore, do not have the capability to reach mental formation. The Sūtra says that, even if they want to look for the practitioner to make offerings to, the *deva maras* (the god demons of mundane love and desire) and the gods themselves cannot even find him – he who transcends the aggregate of perception. For someone with limited meditative concentration, he can sit to slowly calm down his mind until he becomes quiescent, and at that moment, he will feel the lightness of his body and mind. However, thoughts have not been completely shattered. It is because the deep-seated covert lair of the aggregate of mental formation is still there. At any time, when the wind of environmental conditions stirs, mental formation

23

can give rise to the floating bubbles of perception on the surface of the ocean.

When all of the ocean bubbles submerge, the entire surface of the ocean would emerge as quiet and still. However, that ocean surface is the entire aggregate of mental perception; it only needs the wind to rustle, and then, there will be bubbles again. It only needs one agent condition for thoughts to return. We cannot escape this, and this is called *"not having enough meditative concentration power."* Slowly and ever so slowly, when the agent conditions no longer stir, the practitioners will immerse deeply in meditative absorption.

All of our practice exertion at the time being is simply to fool around the outer veil of the aggregate of perception, and we have not yet plunged into the depths of the ocean, and at most, we can only pop those floating bubbles on the ocean surface. For example, there is this one woman whom we used to either detest or love very much. Moreover, although we no longer love or hate her now, it is just as we have incoherently popped the bubbles of emotions on the ocean surface, not even touching the ocean itself.

We must see that many people can be deceptively confused about their realization after they are able to enter into deep absorption. They think that they already attained the fruit of *Arhatship* or become enlightened. This is something that we, as practitioners, need to keep in mind. Otherwise, we would only quiet down a few thoughts, yet already think that we are sublime. In truth, there are people, who through their meditative concentration power are able to suppress the aggregate of perception so that it can temporarily stay calm and be at rest. Perception can also be activated to become an extremely powerful energy; we cannot underrate perception either. Thus, for the practice of *qi-gong*,[2] the practitioners center their *qi* energy into their hands and bodies, and then let the energy flow out of their hands. When they strike with their hands, sounds explode, and that is the vigor of

There are other types of *qi-gong* through which the practitioners can perform astral projection. These practitioners as well as other *qi-gong* practitioners are those who have the accomplishment of sense perception. There are meditation practices in which the master instructs the student "to sit still and let his or her mind reach a state of quiescence, until the time when they can direct their astral projection to go meet such and such a master who will give instructions on this and that." If we continue to sit and use our perception on and on, then one day, we would truly be able to leave our bodies and meet the person whom our teacher had told us about. For example, if our teacher said, "The first person you meet will be a tall gentleman with long, flowing and silver-white hair and beard, and his face blushing like a male angel," then there is no way that you can imagine meeting a person dressed in black. It is because the students achieve the transcendental power of perception, and because the teacher had already pre-given them all the ideas. So they just sit there and rely on their perception until one day, they would mentally encounter a person just like the one their teacher already described, someone with silver-white hair and a

---

[2] Literally: *'life-energy cultivation'* is a centuries-old system of coordinated body-posture and movement, breathing, and meditation used for the purposes of health, spirituality, and martial arts training. With roots in Chinese medicine, philosophy, and martial arts, *qigong* is traditionally viewed by the Chinese and throughout Asia as a practice to cultivate and balance *qi* (pronounced approximately as "*chi*"), translated as *"life energy."* *(www.en.wikipedia.org)*

silver-white beard, tall and handsome, dressed in white, with rosy cheeks just like a male angel. All of that, however, is just a sight of perception that we ourselves have built up.

Everything that we can see, know, understand or discern is all appearances of perception. Even if we can see a real "sky-god," that, too, is just a *"manifestation"* of perception. Perception can create all conditioned objects of consciousness. Thus, even a Buddha whom we can see with our eyes or mind also appears due to our perception, whereas the genuine, authentic Buddha cannot be seen by ordinary eyes. The authentic Buddha does not manifest substantial appearances so that our perception can recognize. The authentic Buddha has no form, and our perception cannot possibly see that which is without form. Perception can only see *"substantiality"* versus *"insubstantiality,"* whereas it cannot possibly see the manifestation in the state of Voidness where there is neither existence nor non-existence. Thus, Voidness is *beyond perception*!

However, when we have not gone beyond perception, all we see is nothing but sense perception, just as we are imagining an elephant, and there is nothing great about that. Discernment is perception, and feeling sad, loved, angry and hatred is also perception, because we perceive things as either substantial or non-substantial. When we grasp both, *"substantiality"* and *"insubstantiality,"* it means that we are being caught in the manifestation of perception. *"Substantiality"* and *"insubstantiality"* are borne by perception. However, when we study deeper, we will comprehend the Buddha's saying that there is no form versus void, because *"form is not different from Void, Void is not different from form,"* and that is a view beyond perception.

Right now, we are being stuck in perception, so to us, *form* is substantial, and *void* is the empty space that does not hold any form. *That*, to us, is *"void."* However, all of this type of discernment is simply perception. All of us are living in, and are being stuck in, perception with no escape route. We have no way to transcend the seeing and knowing that arise from perception. Perception becomes *"cognition;"* it is the knowledge we develop in this life and the discernment between right and wrong. Although we may say all of this is *consciousness*, it simply belongs to the plane of perception and it is not the all-pervading, omniscient knowingness.

Even if all of our thoughts have been settled, and we believe that we have exhausted our practice, then it is not yet utterly completed, because we have only temporarily brought our aggregate of perception to calmness. Although we may abide in meditative absorption for a thousand years, it only means that the aggregate of perception is temporarily being quiescent. That is not the same as attaining sainthood, because there are still the aggregates of mental formation and consciousness that have not been transcended. If the covert lair of mental formation is still intact, then the causal seeds of life-and-death are still intact in their entirety.

So we can see how perception fabricates all sorts of things in our life. We can perceive something as non-existing when it actually exists, yet, when something does not exist, we perceive it as existing. All of the troubles and predicaments in this life come from the spinning of perception. If in this life we can still think of, imagine of, or call to mind something, then all of that is a form of perception. It can actually give rise to great ideologies to provide reasoning for something. All the philosophies and great ideas come from the aggregate of perception.

There are many stories about the workings of perception. We can have perception drawing up even all the way up to seeing the sky-gods, and that, too, can really happen to us. For example, let us say there is a teacher who told us that we have a spirit that follows us, and we come to believe that we truly have an attendant company. When we are sitting by ourselves, we would then hear someone saying something into our ears, and then we would respond to this supposed spirit. Even if we just respond once, that alone can make things worse for us, because it seemed so real that someone is speaking to us. Whoever that spirit is would make a specific comment to us, and we would give a specific response, talking back and forth in a conversation, swinging our legs and waggling our arms around. We think there are two people in this conversation, when in truth, that is purely our own perception. All of these fabricated stories and all the things that we see and hear, we thought of them as being normal, but in reality, they are our perception nonetheless.

There was an experiment on the practice exertion of perception that took place in the United Kingdom, possibly in 1979. It was clearly shown on a television program. While sitting, this person perceived the metal bar in front of him had become bent. At that time, whatever was metal under the influence of his perception all got bent. Anything metal in the television station, including metal bars of the television set also became bent. This person exerted his power of perception in such a way. Or for example, if we detest the person sitting next to us, we perceive him having a stomachache. If we have some power, then all of a sudden, that person would have a stomachache. People like hypnotists, and black magicians all have the great inner mind's power and the power of their perception can arouse a thought that would make another person act according to what they perceive. The hypnotists and black magicians themselves have to experience quite deep meditative absorption in their practice in order to have this kind of power.

Therefore, everything that happens in life, including our suffering and happiness, are produced by perception. When someone curses at us, it is not a big deal, but we go on having perception about it for a while. Then later on, we feel tormented, and we cry in resentment, feeling frustrated and self-pity. It is because we perceive ourselves as an important figure in society, and when people are denigrating us, no longer putting us on the pedestal, it leads us to suffering. Or perhaps some young fellow belittled us, saying "You are nobody, yet you think you are so important." We would cry, and choke with anger, because what he said destroyed our perception as such and such a person.

For all of us who are existing here in this world, we believe that we are this figure and that figure. We think this body and this mind belong to us. This way of thinking is borne out of perception. Gradually, we become attached and we grasp; we frame ourselves in a certain status. Ultimately, when people say things that put us out of our current position or people misunderstand our status, then we suffer. For example, we perceive ourselves as intellectual people or scholars, yet people criticize us and belittle us, then we suffer. All of that is determined by our contrived thinking, and when people shatter it, we feel agitated. However, all of that belongs to perception and nothing else. Existing things turn non-existing, non-existing things turn existing, small things turn big, and big things turn small – all of that simply manifests due to our perception.

In life, we always perceive things as real. When people talk to each other, we also think it is real, but all of that is simply our perception. Perception is illusive. In reality, this body is also an illusion, this mind is an illusion and this life is an illusion. When we accept that we are having a body, that is accepting perception. When we see something as real, it means it is real within our perception but not genuinely so in the realm of truth.

That which is *"reality"* is utterly different, whereas what we see as real or unreal in a mundane sense that arises from perception. Furthermore, when we see true versus fake, right versus wrong, good versus bad, retained versus lost, existing versus non-existing, immobile versus moving, proper versus improper, short versus tall... in this mundane world, then that is *"the seeing of perception."* Nevertheless, that which is *reality* does not have right or wrong, good or bad, internal or external, up or down, short or tall. Therefore, we have fallen into, and are stuck in, perception and unable to get out.

When we think that this belief or this thought in and of itself is *"our selves,"* then *"that thinking"* by and of itself is also perception. Perception wraps up nearly everything in our life. If we see all phenomena that happen in our life as either real or unreal, existing or non-existing, then all of that is perception. Perception weaves illusion into our life, but it is not *"reality."* Therefore, when reality emerges, then all those illusions will disappear; body, mind, understanding, and knowledge will also disappear, and that which remains is simply the *vivid presence of reality,* immaculate, empty-hollow and quiescent. This reality is the living force, so stupendous, so amazingly marvelous. At the time being, ordinary human beings do not have enough capability to fathom a single *"mental thought"* in a most profound way. Therefore, all of us simply *"perceive with delusion."* Here, we can even say that we *"perceive perception with delusion"* and all this life is but a *"delusion of thoughts."*

Whether a wise and learned person or a dull person, whether an ordinary person or a person with high social status, they all appoint themselves through their perception. But for an awakened person with a brilliant, clear view, there is nothing that is either high or low, and there is only that which is either in accordance with the truth or mistaken from the truth. *"The truth"* herein refers to the True Sign of all phenomena, which is Signlessness – Voidness, rather than the relative truth in a dualistic cycle. Thus, to be in accordance with the truth means to be emancipated from illusion, and to be mistaken about the truth means to accept illusion. The very fact that we are *"delusive"* is because we erroneously become mislead by our thoughts, and that is all! The day we no longer are deluded with this concept – meaning to *identify* ourselves with illusion – then our body and mind will dissipate, and the external circumstances altogether can no longer affix to us. Thus, as far as all of the activities in this life are concerned, if we cannot see to their very depths, which are Signlessness – Voidness, then it looks like we have already fallen into perception. Perception, therefore, is far-flung and not at all simple.

The aggregate of mental formation (karmic formation)

Mental formation is the covert lair that constructs our self-grasping, seeing *"ourselves"* as different from everything else around us. Why are we seeing that there are our *"selves"*? In the twelve links of dependent origination, we talk about ignorance and how it makes contact with mental formation. Ignorance does not mean total darkness, but it is the inability to see the existing reality, immaculate, empty and tranquil. That is called ignorance.

Right now we are seeing and hearing with our sense faculties, and that is considered being ignorant. How can we call it ignorance when our eyes see forms and our ears hear sounds? Because seeing forms is falling into sense perception, hearing sounds is falling into sense perception, and seeing dualistically right versus wrong is falling into the deep-seated stratum of ignorance. If in this very presence, we fail to recognize the reality and the existent pure and luminous *Suchness* as the *Perfect All-Transcendent Wisdom,* then it means we already fell into the level of ignorance. Therefore, if we do not have the capability to immerse in our *"inherently pure true nature"* and in *Prajñā* with every passing moment that manifests right here, then we already fell into the depths of ignorance.

Therefore, ignorance does not necessarily mean darkness. Ignorance is, matter-of-factly, obscurity, and herein, obscurity means *the inability to recognize genuinely the existent truth, the true existence, the reality in this pristine presence.* If, in some moments, the practitioner realizes that this very vivid presence is altogether *Prajñā*, he or she will then be emancipated from ignorance. This very existence is *Prajñā*, and every activity and movement in this life is indeed *Prajñā*. *Prajñā* gives birth to all movements, and thus, all movements are, indeed, *Prajñā*. Once we come to terms with it and thoroughly see it, we are liberated from ignorance.

So by then, it means ignorance does not make contact with anything whatsoever, because *Prajñā* is simply this very vivid presence, not slightly before or after. Whatever we see turns out to be the very pristine presence. This mental moment is the presence; the next mental instant is the presence, and the very presence is the empty reality, hollow, pure, unobstructed, and illuminating without confusion-delusion. Sense perception, mental formation and consciousness would all dissolve into this clear, luminous pristine presence. Seeing it in such a way is actually *Prajñā;* it is the same as seeing the intrinsic essence of the five aggregates as being Void. However, at the time being, we do not have this capability; we see that there is existence and non-existence, good and bad, form and sound, etc. and it means that we have fallen into the deep level of ignorance where mental formation eventually comes into play.

Since we have an erroneous view and see things with delusion, then it is this delusion that leads to other delusions, and hundreds of thousands of other delusions will manifest. Delusion is not simply just one instance of seeing or one instance of hearing, but within a diminutive mental instant, there are countless delusions of ours. They have never stopped, even temporarily.

From one thing to many things, absolutely everything, indeed, is enthralled by, and arises from, multitudes of mental kernels in our consciousness. All of these delusions are the causal seeds that give birth to new delusions, and they create new causes leading to new fruitions uninterruptedly. All of these conti-nuums become ever so abundant in our mind, and this is what we call mental formation. The workings of mental formation is intensively forceful, never just a simple, unremarkable continua-tion in our mindstream.

When we look at the vast ocean, we see waves coming into shore with round bubbles, or when we see sea foams in the middle of the ocean, these bubbles or sea forms can be the analogies of sense perception. The scriptures say that within one single eye blink, there are twenty great thoughts, and each great thought contains 16,798,000 cycles of arising and ceasing; therefore, within one eye blink there are infinite billions and billions of thought-cycles of arising and ceasing. When a thought surfaces, it already has turned into a perception. However, within the sphere of mental formation, a thought does not appear in its entirety. Mental formation is just like in a humongous heap of rice stalks where you only need a few seedlings as the agent producers. It takes as little as one in a billion mental formations to produce a perception. Perception is only a tiny portion of a billion exponentials of mental formation, and that is why perception is extremely diminutive when compared to mental formation.

Therefore, that which we are currently seeing and knowing is exceedingly minuscule. Worldly knowledge is only a portion of a billionth in a multi-billion exponentials of mental formation. The scientists discovered something today and will discover some-thing else tomorrow, but all the [discoveries and] ideologies that were founded thus far are so insignificantly small when compared to mental formation. Science cannot even "fully" decode one DNA in the human body, whereas each person has millions upon millions of DNA like that. Scientists do not have enough research information to write up even a portion of a billion of the DNA in our bodies.

Mental formation gives birth to sense perception. It is mental formation that is closely connected with the DNA in our bodies; therefore, the "brain" of DNA is a billion in a billion exponentials more intelligent than our own brain. Our thinking and discernment are insignificantly small when compared to the awestruck "brain" of our DNA. This brain can be truly frightening! The scientists up until now have not had the ability to *fully* decipher one single DNA. For example, when speaking of genetic inheritance, if the father has a specific DNA, then his child is only able to emit a code that is modestly equivalent to his father's, just to show that there is something equipollent in a father and child biological blood relation. The scientists could not explain it all, and they only knew that there are some minor vibrations or transmittance which corresponds between father and child.

Until now, the physical body of a human is something very miraculous, and science is not yet able to sufficiently speak of one single DNA. To be able to see the activities of one single cell is already something extremely complicated that science cannot explain wholly – it can only translate into the language of intracellular and extracellular which include *natri, magie, kali* and *cancil*. If the intracellular is lacking *natri* or *magie*, it will give rise to the kinds of vibration that would affect our brain waves, which lead to the distortion in our thinking. However, all of that is purely external research.

Apparently, the basis of our thinking's distortion is from the aggregate of mental formation and not from this little brain of ours. Mental formation emits signals which the aggregate of perception receives, albeit inaccurately. The aggregate of perception is the blood child of the aggregate of mental formation; our brain is the blood child of the aggregate of perception. In other words, the aggregate of perception is the product of the aggregate of mental formation, and our brain is the product of the aggregate of perception. Therefore, our paternal grandfather is the aggregate of mental formation, which gives birth to our father, the aggregate of perception, which in turn gives birth to our talking and activities in this life, and that is us. We are the last product in this line of productivity. All of our activities, whether it is talking, standing, walking, or feeling loved, angry, or hateful are all born from the aggregate of perception. The aggregate of perception was conceived by the aggregate of mental formation; thus, the aggregate of mental formation is the covert lair and the very deep-rooted foundation from which this life stems.

It is only with this Buddhist point of view that we can discover the root source. Just like a person who immerses deeply in meditation absorption, he or she can see the place of origin of the aggregate of mental formation, which is indeed the birthplace of sense perception, which in turn gives birth to life. If perception is dismantled, then at that moment, we no longer see a body and mind. It means that although we still carry a body, it will completely lose its density. The aggregate of perception is what makes us substantially heavy; it makes us feel that there is a self, a body of however many kilograms, a mind, and an arm raising and dropping.

Yet, it is the aggregate of mental formation that generates our volition which gives rise to our thoughts. For example, we may not be able to make it if we have to sit here for an hour, yet, it is the force of the aggregate of mental formation which utilizes volition in order for us to end up being able to sit here for that long. The exertion for us to sit here is mental formation. Another example is of a wounded person in the battlefield. Apparently, he has no more energy to even walk, but he exerts himself and drags himself back to his place, and the moment someone sees him, he faints. The volition for him to drag his crippled body back home is the aggregate of mental formation.

All inner efforts to construct and to maintain the deep-seated "*self*" come from the aggregate of mental formation and _not_ from perception. The aggregate of perception only implements what is emitted from the aggregate of mental formation. Our thoughts, however, are very slow and frail and so they cannot decipher all the cues that are sent out by the aggregate of mental formation. Because they cannot decode fully, they become blind, and are unable to see to the very depths of the root of mental formation. There are a number of people who say that they can see the aggregate of mental formation, but this way of talking is without proper understanding, because if they have not had any experiential, deep meditative absorption, they would not have enough wisdom insight to see the aggregate of mental formation. Even if we simply want to see the surface of mental formation, that, too, requires us to least once enter a very deep level of meditative absorption.

Normally when we speak of the aggregate of mental formation, it is just for us to arbitrarily have some ideas, when in reality, we do not really have enough wisdom and spiritual power to be able to see the aggregate of mental formation. Even the gods cannot see the aggregate of mental formation, and the gods of the Heaven of the Thirty-Three do not even know which way to prowl. In the past, when I gave the discourses on the *Śūraṅgama Sūtra* and especially on the section of transcending the aggregate of perception, I wanted to emphasize the fact that] the five aggregates should not be seen as the "five *maras* of the aggregates," but rather as the fifty states of realization experienced by a practitioner. Even if the gods want to make offerings to such practitioners – those who have dismantled the aggregate of perception and already reached mental formation – the gods would not be able to do so. It is because these practitioners no longer leave any trace in this mundane world.

Thus, there are various secret *mantras* that can be used to settle the aggregate of perception so that the person sitting next to us cannot see our physical bodies. Many people are still utilizing these invisibility spell *mantras*; they can swiftly influence and settle aggregate of perception so that the person sitting next to them cannot see them. However, that is only to resolve our sense perception, whereas the aggregate of mental formation is something that is immensely vast. A bubble in the middle of the ocean is sense perception, and the enormous ocean itself is mental formation. Therefore, can you imagine how difficult it is to dismantle the aggregate of mental formation? Our competitiveness, adverse opposition, affirmation and rejection all belong to the manifestations of perception. It does not matter whether there are appearances of perception or not, perception is simply superficial and it only covers the surface of the vast ocean while mental formation fills the entire ocean.

Once the force of mental formation actuates, we would not be able to even imagine what it is like. Therefore, a person who can transcend perception and act upon his mental formation will most likely have supranatural powers. For example, when someone in his deep sleep falls into the level of the unconscious mind, his perception becomes deeply settled, his mental formation is actuated, and he can actually walk on the walls as he would on the ground. He can even walk on the wall with his head pointing down without falling. If he wants to flutter and fly like a bird, that would be a normal thing, too, because his perception is already exhausted and he is using his body as that of a bird.

I also remember once upon a time there was a neighborhood friend of mine who sleep-walked in the middle of the night. When sleepwalking, he rushed out of the house even though the door was closed, like a mouse getting through a hole. His whole family opened the door and chased after him. He flew over the ditch just like a bird. After circling around, he flew back to the house, slipped back inside the mosquito net and felt back asleep. As for these sleepwalkers, we cannot possibly imagine the kind of power they have; it is as if they possess many transmundane powers.

There is also story that I always like to tell. At that time in the countryside in Vietnam, when the foreign invaders engaged in a raid, they would take everything and anything. There was an eighty year old woman, and as she heard people howl, "Oh, Grandma Hai! The invaders are raiding," she raced to the pigsty, picked up a pig that weighted over 100 kilograms and darted back outside. After running for a while, she became overly exhausted and collapsed. How in the world could that old lady pick up a pig that weighted over 100 kilograms, do we know? That is due to the force of mental formation.

There was another man who, as he heard of the invaders coming to raid, panicked and did not know which way to run for his life, because the soldiers would shoot if they saw people running. So he dashed into a nearby thorny bush to hide, and when everything was over, he became conscious again and saw that he was completely covered with prickling thorns. He then screamed for other villagers to come to rescue him, and they had to cut down the thorny branches to slowly pull him out. As mental formation activates, we can do things beyond our imagination, as perception cannot keep up at that moment.

As mental formation appears so abruptly, perception does not have enough time to catch up with it. Whatever is superbly speedy belongs to mental formation. Therefore, for the Zen masters to converse and answer questions so briskly without having to rely on any thinking based on sense perception, then that is the activation of mental formation. Those masters have glided beyond the level of the aggregate of perception, and thus, even materials would not be able to impede them.

Whatever that is so brisk, agile and precise is all activated by the aggregate of mental formation. Our intuition, therefore, belongs to mental formation. When we look at a person, if we intuitively know not through analytical thinking whether he or she is good or bad, that this is a part of mental formation. On the one hand, if we rely on our analysis looking at this person's physical signs, eyes, ears, tone of voice and facial features... to decide what these signs embody, sincere or not sincere, then it would take perception a whole day to figure it out. On the other hand, the aggregate of mental formation can just glide through and already know how this person actually is inside out. That which is penetrating, powerful, swift, sharp, accurate, and sensitive in this life all belongs to the level of the aggregate of mental formation.

Therefore, when we become less imprudently agitated, then we would be more intelligent. For example, if they ask us one question and we can answer immediately without thinking, then that is the workings of the aggregate of mental formation; or when we can figure out or solve some issues immediately while another person would take a whole time and still cannot figure it out. On the other hand, when people challenge us with some questions, and we can immediately give brisk, exact answers without having to think about them, then it means that we do not rely on the aggregate of perception. In cases like that, it means that we are not going through the baggage of stereotype, knowledge, memories, and typical learning, and we do not compare, calculate, and deliberately consider between this and that. It is precisely due to this that our seeing becomes very accurate. This seeing is actually called our intuition. Occasionally, if perception is settled, intuition will surface. Intuition is actually the very sharp discriminating mind, but it is still being caught at the level of mental formation.

The aggregate of mental formation is, therefore, something that is very profound. Once it actuates, it would be impossible for us to determine anything in advance. There are a number of masters on the path who have at least once gone beyond the aggregate of mental formation, which means they have experienced *"the five aggregates being Void,"* and their way of communication, thereby, does not require any thinking, because they have already transcended the level of sense perception. They no longer need to use perception, because the root source of the aggregate of mental formation is limitless. The treasure of mental formation is infinite.

During the phase when we do not yet have enough wisdom to go beyond the aggregate of mental formation, we have to utilize the aggregate of perception, which is so slow and diminutive, but once we transcend perception, we will never exhaust the foundational power of mental formation. Even just a single cell of ours is capable of transmitting enough mental power for us to utilize for ten-thousand lives, let alone all the cells in our bodies. One miniscule mental time interval of the aggregate of mental formation is enough to actuate all of the activities in our life. All of these thought-arisings become the mental power to maintain, preserve, multiply and produce a new life force, and that is the aggregate of mental formation.

Therefore, our life arises from the root of mental formation.

Nevertheless, it is never easy for us to see the aggregate of mental formation. If for once we can see mental formation then it means we already see to the very core of our life-and-death cycle. We can utterly dismantle mental formation when we penetrate this very root source. It is not, however, due to our practice exertion or through our imagination of *"the five aggregates being Void"* that we are able to extirpate mental formation. It is not at all like that. All of our life activities comprise of sense faculties and sense objects coming into contact with one another followed by the discriminating consciousness making comparisons, etc. It is similar to how the *manas* consciousness amasses the *karmic* seeds and deposits them into the storage. Our mental formation stocks up *karmic* seeds similarly to the *Ālaya* consciousness. From the Mind-Only School's point of view, the aggregate of mental formation functions similarly and it has the capability to set up the foundation not just for one life but for countless lives.

Therefore, first, we talk about entering the womb, which is the same as *"ignorance coming into contact with mental formation,"* then comes the moment when we leave this physical body, form, sensation, perception, mental formation and consciousness will still be intact. Overall, the period of living when we are still alive is considered the first intermediate state, and the period following our death can be considered the second intermediate state. The mental body in the intermediate state also cognizes, understands, differentiates, and feels sad, loved, angry and hateful; this mental body also discerns between happiness and sadness just like how we are functioning in our present physical bodies. There is not a slight change whatsoever between this intermediate state and when we are alive except for one thing, and that is we no longer carry a body of fifty kilograms in this state and that is it. Other than that, we are not at all different from how we are now.

When we face with disheartening incidents, all we want is to die in order to end our grief, but even if we die, our sadness cannot be extinguished! Because after we commit suicide, we then realize at that moment that we remain exactly the same, and there is no way that we can escape this grief. After we die, whomever we love, miss, are bothered with, or are angry with, will be even brighter and clearer. Because right now, we still have to carry our physical bodies so this physicality somewhat puts a veil on our suffering or happiness, but once the material body is left behind, everything will appear more obvious.

We are trapped in the body of five aggregates, unable to get out, and even if we want to end our suffering, we do not have a way. We cannot possibly resolve our suffering if we cannot disintegrate our body of five aggregates; therefore, the Buddha taught that the five aggregates must be Void in order to transcend all miseries. Since we are stuck in this body, birth and death in this life are merely changes of the physical body or the aggregate of form, and if so, then it does not really carry any special meaning other than that. It does not matter how many causes and effects, how much love, and how much resentment we have – they are all contained in the aggregate of mental formation. It stores all of the causal seeds of life-and-death. No matter how many causal seeds there are, they are all placed in the aggregate of mental formation. Infinite lives in the past and infinite lives ready to be formed in the future are all stocked up in the aggregate of mental formation. Thus, it is never easy to resolve this aggregate. Although one may enter meditative absorption for a hundred years, one can still be trapped in the cycle of life-and-death, because one has not yet been able to resolve the covert lair of the aggregate of mental formation. What a terribly horrible thing.

43

Now let us go back to *"ignorance coming into contact with mental formation"* so that we can see how we are being trapped. We do not have a way to escape sensation, sense perception, mental formation and consciousness. There is no one who has the ability to break out; even if we bring the Buddha to mind or recite the *mantra,* we still cannot flee from the aggregate of mental formation. Unless we can find a way so that mental formation and consciousness can transform into Void, then we can clear out. So it means that if the five aggregates have not yet become Void, no one can break free from the cycle of life-and-death. Don't falsely perceive and don't dream on; however, many people dreamingly imagine that they only need to recite the Buddha's name a few times, and they would take rebirth in such and such a realm. That is merely daydreaming and not reality. If we want to transcend life-and-death, we must practice so that the five aggregates can become *"exhausted"* in order to be emancipated from the cycle of life-and-death, and only that is the actual truth. This is the very core of what the Buddha taught.

The Buddha said very clearly that if the five aggregates are not yet Void, then suffering still exists in its entirety. Even after we leave our bodies now, the "new" five aggregates would come into being. There will be a *density-less* form substance, and if we can somehow measure and weigh something that has no density, it will still appear in its own form. After one leaves his body, for example, one's perception still perceives himself as Mr. A. Prior to leaving the body, perception already registered everything as such, and thus, perception brought this pre-registered appearance into the intermediate realm. In the intermediate realm, he will still be Mr. A with two arms, two legs, and a normal head, and that is just like him before he passed away. Therefore, it is perception that formulates the "new" person in the afterlife. This person will have all the emotions of sadness, love, anger and aversion intact, including all the knowledge that he had accumulated in the preceding life, and even knowledge from other past lives, too.

During our current life, this body of ours was borne from our mother and father; therefore, we only operate with the segment of life that has been registered by our physical brain in that specific life. However, if we stop using this body and the brain-registered life segment of this life, we can thoroughly fathom all the way into our past lives. The perception and mental registry we have in about eighty years in this life is just like a movie; we can call it part one, and part two is our next life. After we leave this physical body, our seeing can thoroughly penetrate without impediments. At that moment, we can see how such and such a person had played a prank on us a few hundred lives ago and where he is living now. We can see everything in its entirety; therefore, all the sadness, love, anger and aversion will clearly appear, even more obvious than at the time being. Right now (when we are still living), it is just a thought, but at that moment (after we leave the body), all appearances would take shape very vividly, such as how he had slashed us, how many of our tendons were cut, what unbearable pain we went through, how we bled and how we died. All of that may have happened ten lives ago, but after we leave our bodies, we can see that, for example, he is currently sitting over there, and we can see everything very clearly.

After we leave this body, we will be seven times more intelligent than as of now, and even if you want to say it is seven hundred times more so, then you can put it that way, too, too. Everything will be crystal clear; everything that happened in the cycle of life-and-death will become unobstructed through our seeing as they are not interrupted or broken up into segments. On the other hand, right now in our lives, our seeing is being interrupted and broken up into segments. It is because our brain only starts to register beginning at the age of four; but prior to that, it is quite empty because our mental registry has not operated yet. Thus, the segment of the beginning of our life is vague.

After we leave the intermediate state to enter the womb to take rebirth again, we can penetrate the obscured stage in the womb through meditation absorption. When we are in the intermediate state, all of this life's activities are still intact, and then we will begin to recall all of these activities starting at the zero age, then up to one year old and etc. It only needs a few eye blinks for us to completely know all of our preceding life, and a few more eye blinks to know who we were in a past life, what our practice level was, or how far we had progressed with our practice exertion. We would be able to know of all those details. Whichever *karmas* are the most powerful and the nearest will appear first; then, anything that is related to the *karma* of the consecutive life will then appears, so that the aggregate of mental formation can begin to calculate based on these data. Actually, it does not need to really calculate anything, because it is superlative to the point that no computer can ever collect all the information as rapidly as the aggregate of mental formation.

For example, when we prepare to form a new life, the first *karmic* event which shall happen at age one in the new life might be the result of something which happened eight lives ago, and at age two, another event might be caused by something which happened five hundred lives ago. Then, that which shall happen at age three might be caused by something which happened a few billion lives ago, and at age twenty, it might be caused by something which happened a thousand lives ago. It means that the *karmic* happenings in the new life do not manifest in an orderly fashion. In actuality, the *entirety of the minuscule segments of our own thoughts* would all be gathered by the aggregate of mental formation so that they can form our new life in just an eye blink. It is that speedy! Thus, the aggregate of mental formation is something that can transcend all of space, time, as well as matter. That is why some people can walk on electrical wires during sleepwalking and never are electrocuted, because during that time they are living in the aggregate of mental formation.

Therefore, it means that during the existence of the mental body in the intermediate state, the individual still uses sense perception, mental formation and consciousness, but he will not be able to utilize mental formation. This is something very interesting about life-and-death. The aggregate of perception will activate the life of the mental body, leading it to move about freely in the world without gross matter. However, in reality, to say that it is utterly *without matter* is not correct; it is still a form of matter, but *subtle* matter. The mental body can travel freely everywhere, except the Vajra Seat of the Buddha, and it cannot penetrate the womb of a mother. It is as if this mental body has supramundane power, because aside from those two places, we can move about everywhere freely and at ease after death. There is no need to spend money for airline tickets, yet we can go on traveling from place to place very comfortably. It is even faster than the airplane because we only need to generate one thought, then we would already have arrived in America or another country.

Therefore, to die is not the end! Being dead can be much happier than being alive right now if we are "not convicted" of any unwholesome deeds, especially if we have a mind of clarity until the last phase. The moment we leave our bodies, the positive and negative *karmas* will flock in. If we are sufficiently self-collected and calm when we are flooded with all of our *karmas* before leaving our bodies, then they will self-dissolve the moment they bore down on us. The non-virtuous *karmas* will rapidly sweep us away, but if we are adequately settled and unruffled, they will all disappear, a boundlessly spacious expanse will manifest and it is the beginning of our freedom. What is worrisome though is that we may not have enough meditative absorption when the virtuous and non-virtuous *karmas* flock in, and they would sweep us away, no longer knowing where we are standing. That is when the powerful winds of *karma* blow us away. However, wherever *karma* would lead us has already been worked out by our mental formation.

The moment we leave our body of flesh and bones, a mental interval which contains all the virtuous and non-virtuous *karmas* would appear, and then we would return to being normal again, but the orientation of our next life, driven by our *karmic* habitual tendencies, will continue to lead us on without halting. We use the term *"halting"* but in reality, we would not come to a standstill in the same way we are sitting well composed here. If we do not have meditative absorption at that time, we would not be able to compose ourselves and sit still like right now.

However, if we are self-collected and are not swept away by our virtuous and non-virtuous *karmas*, then we can freely travel at ease in the expanse of spaciousness. This expanse is one with great freedom; we can freely stand, walk, sit, lie down, engage in activities or abide wherever according to our wish. This means that we are utterly free of any so-called *"conviction."* However, we are still Mr. Nguyen Van A, Ms. Nguyen Thi Mit, or Mr. Nguyen Van Xoai; we have not yet emancipated from these imprints, because we still exist in that level of perception. It is because we cannot yet dispel our perception, and thus, we have not yet removed ourselves from our past life's engraved impressions.

These imprints still prescribe us to be, for example, Mr. Nguyen Van A, the husband of Mrs. Nguyen Thi B. After Mr. A died, he left behind his heritage, and following that, his wife left with another man, taking with her all of his possession. So Mr. A was enraged, and he struck her, but she did not feel any pain, because his mental thinking has nothing to do with her physical body, even if he hit her out of bitter jealousy. The mental body knows it all and sees it all, but it cannot impinge on matter if it does not have any power from practice exertion. Although he may get angry, scream and yell, jump around, or feel resentful and hateful, his wife and the living people around him will be completely unaware of it.

Due to the fact that the aggregate of perception continues to perceive ourselves as who we were in our immediate past life, we can continue to exist as such a person in that intermediate realm. Then, when the father and mother, who are the approaching conditions of our next life, appear, we would feel a triangular force of *karma*. When our father and mother are in union, they generate a fire of lust. At that moment, infinite, countless consciousnesses of other beings crowd around, including consciousnesses of non-humans, who also try to rush in. We, too, become their rivals, competing with them to come on board. If we have practiced well, then automatically, we have a force that all of the other consciousnesses succumb to, and thus, it helps us to enter the mother's womb quite easily. If we choose a specific couple as our parents, then no one can compete with us. However, if we do not have any spiritual force but only *karma,* then through the force of *karma,* there will be a cord that automatically sucks us into the womb of a mother, and we cannot possibly resist it.

Being whirled by the intense force of *karma*, we cannot possibly resist it, and thus, we would be sucked by it and end up banging against the uterus wall of our mother. We would go through a fleeting moment of shock, and completely lose all of our cognition. We end up not knowing anything anymore. Whatever stipulates us as Mr. Nguyen Van A utterly extinguishes at that very moment. After we passed away, the self-grasping notion of us as being Mr. Nguyen Van A did not die out until now. This is what the mundane world would call "to eat the rice porridge of senile dementia," and as such, we would end up with "no knowledge" of our past lives whatsoever. This is the case of the intermediate state where we were thrusted into the uterus wall too violently, and thus, makes us lose all of our knowledge of being Mr. Nguyen Van A in the last life. The "force of *karma*" creates an awestruck, dreadful panic; it is not just an ordinary pull.

We can imagine ourselves sitting here, and all of a sudden being pulled away instantaneously for a thousand kilometers within a minute – how horrifying that would be! However, by comparison, the gravitational pull into our mother's womb is a million times more forceful. In an eye blink, we would be yanked into our mother's womb by a vigorous force of gravity, and as we hear a "crashing noise," everything becomes pitch-black and our cognition ceased. Those of us who had fallen unconscious would be able to have some ideas about this; the moment we faint, everything is pitch-black, and then afterward, we would regain our cognition. However, in the case of being pulled into the mother's womb, there would be no cognition that returns to us after we wake up. That is indeed ignorance, because there would not be enough time for us to compare, to choose, to take it or to leave it. It is impossible for us to do anything because of the pulling force of *karma.* Therefore, the force of *karma* is truly horrid, especially the *karma* of the cycle of birth and death.

Thus, while being frantically in chaos and in gross darkness, there is the wavering and pulling force that gives our consciousness rattling fright. Just imagine the engine of an airplane flying about ten kilometers above the ground suddenly shuts down and the plane takes a plunge from the sky above. Such gravitational force would make anyone trying to survive absolutely terrified. Alternatively, we can also image ourselves jump off a twenty-meter high building; that very moment is terribly horrifying, too.

Following that moment of terribly frightful, impenetrable blackness, let us now talk about the *"self,"* the *"silent, latent self"* of ours. First, our aggregate of perception becomes over-whelmingly panic-stricken, not knowing what to do; it can no longer perceive existence nor non-existence. Since perception is now being in the dark, mental formation actuates. After being whirled into the pitch-black womb by the force of *karma,* our incessant self-grasping does not accept that it is now vanishing into the chaos and pitch-black physical space, and so it tries to regain its focus and calmness. In the physical space inside the mother's womb, our consciousness stumbles and gropes.

The moment the ovum and the sperm meet together, there is a flicker of light, and thus, our consciousness is gladdened, tenaciously clings to the mother's ovum. Where there is the trio of ovum, sperm, and consciousness, then the embryo is conceived. While clinging to the ovum, the aggregate of mental formation begins to generate its vigor, constructing a new life in less than a finger snap. No matter whether the *karmas* are from five lives ago, or a hundred, eight thousand, two to three million, or five to seven thousand million lives ago, the aggregate of mental formation would collect them all from these past lives and pump them into a new life, lining up all of them through steps one, two, three, four, five, etc. and getting everything ready for us for our approaching life. Whether we will be a boy or a girl, with dark or fair skin, short or tall, skinny or heavy, all of these details will all be worked out by mental formation. It would work through an extended period of causes and effects, gather them together, filter, sift, and thrust all of them into the new life in less than a finger snap. That is *"ignorance coming into contact with mental formation."*

After mental formation finishes determining the entire new life, which is ready to come into being, the conservation of our individuality will now begin. Now we will become *something*, and we are no longer the good old Mr. Nguyen Van A. We are the ovum, and the ovum is actually the being of our life. It will be the start of the discernment of consciousness, and we will compare and distinguish that there is a *"self"* right here. Of course, in this segment of our existence in the womb, we are still in the dark; however, if we have meditative absorption, then we would be able to clearly perceive the sphere of our existence in the womb.

These days, science was able to photograph the hearts of practitioners in sitting meditation; their hearts are amazingly bright. Similarly, the wisdom of the people, while in the womb, who have cultivated good practice, is much more lucid than that of non-practitioners. That is why after these practitioners enter life again, they are intelligent and knowledgeable, because they are being lead and guided by wisdom. Mental formation makes plan in accordance with the approaching life. Once this life is gone, then the *karmic* imprints of the preceding life get their priorities and are much stronger. Actually, it is the aggregate of mental formation that attracts various *karmic* causes and effects of the preceding life, and amasses these old *karmas* into the new life.

At that moment, we spontaneously regain our consciousness following our being obscured in the dark, and slowly start to see that *"there is a self"* again. Although *"there is a self,"* this *"self"* is not at all similar to anything else around us. When we first recognize that we are completely unlike anything around us, that is the first moment when *"self-grasping"* becomes revitalized. When we see that we are dissimilar to everything, it means our *"individual selves"* become well-formed. This is exactly when *"ignorance comes into contact with mental formation, and mental formation comes into contact consciousness."* At this point in time, our consciousness can only differentiate between hot and cold. If our mother eats or drinks something cold, then we would feel cold, and if our mother eats or drinks something hot, then we would feel hot. The fluctuation of our mother has a direct influence on us, but if our power of meditative absorption is strong, then we can counter affect our mother. This is the interaction between the *karmic* habitual tendencies of mother and child.

Why is it that a mother gives birth to a child with deformities? It is not due to our mother, but due to us. It is due to the workings of mental formation and because we had established some causes and effects in past lives. Due to the *karma* of the fetus, it leads the mother to having the desire to follow a certain unhealthy diet or detrimental habits during her pregnancy, so the child would end up with a health issue or a deformity. It is also ourselves who generate the influencing *karma* that leads our mother to crave for a certain food or to follow certain undesirable habit, so that we would be born mentally disarranged, incognizant, unintelligent, or with cancer after birth. If we do not have those kinds of *karma,* then our mother would not have any desire for any of those things during her pregnancy.

We can also clearly see the said point in a story during Buddha's lifetime. At that time, when Sāriputra was still in the womb,

Sāriputra's mother came to be so brilliant. Her own younger brother, Śramana Dirghanakha, was a famed Vedic commentator in India at that time who surpassed everyone in debate. However, when Sāriputra was still in utero, Śramana Dirghanakha lost to his sister at least a hundred times in public. He was afraid that after his nephew was born, he would lose to him over debate, too, and thus, he went to live in the forest spending many months and years searching for answers that he even forgot to cut this fingernails. Due to his long fingernails, people called him Dirghanakha ("Long Nails") – a *Brahmacarin* with long nails. Therefore, when we are still in the womb, we can *influence* our mother if we have a vigorous force.

There was a woman from Tiền Giang (a province in southern Vietnam) who had an ectopic pregnancy. She followed the brown rice nutritional macrobiotic diet #7 for a short while, and then, the viable embryo entered inside the uterus and everything became normal afterward. While continuing to follow the nutritional diet #7, she craved for a bowl of beef noodle soup, and after eating it, she went insane. Her family had to bring her to the mental institute. After I heard about this, I told her to rub her stomach and to tell her unborn child that she was very sorry, and that she promised from that time onward until the time she gave birth to him, she would never eat meat again, all along asking for his forgiveness. After she did what I told her, she became clear-headed again and she went home. Her young son is now ten years old. These days, whenever he sees any ladies selling fish on the streets, he would sit around to give them a Dharma talk. He would go on talking until the sellers overturn the fish baskets to release the fish into the water. If they refuse to do that, then he would refuse to get up and leave, and continues to talk back and forth about cause and effect.

Thus, it means that while we are still in the womb, our vigor can influence our mother. If the mother eats well and engages in proper activities during pregnancy, then a person with great merits will enter the embryo. However, someone without merits who has the *karma* to have illnesses or disabilities in this lifetime, then the aggregate of mental formation would work it out priorly. It would influence the mother so that she would engage in improper activities or eating habits during her pregnancy, so that the person would be born half paralyzed, crippled, armless, or blind, etc.

I remember how one time, a mother brought her eighteen year old daughter to see me. This young lady was very beautiful but she cannot speak the human language. Once in while she would howl and the screeching sound was horrifying, making us feel as if we were in the hell realm. The mother said that during her pregnancy, she drank a few litters of sugary lemon juice on a daily basis, causing the brain of this young girl to be completely ruined. Therefore, if we were to just take a look at a certain period of time, such as during the mother's pregnancy, then it looks as if it was due to the mother's improper eating habits. However, it was actually due to our *karma* that our mother could not resist these habits otherwise. Thus, we should not put the blame on our mother, but it actually comes from our own *karma* and influence.

When *"ignorance comes into contact with mental formation,"* mental formation amasses all the *karmas* from thousands of thousands of lives ago and thrusts them all into one single life. Should there be some kind of interdependent relationships that would bring about certain happenings during a certain period in our life, then the aggregate of mental formation will meticulously arrange for our mother to eat, drink and engage in activities n a certain way in order to give birth to us in a certain way in our new life. This new life is also the groundwork of the aggregate of mental formation. For each step in our activities in this life, for example, we may think that we are the ones who make the decisions and select this major or that major to study in college, who think we like to do this or to do that, or who think that we have the abilities to make a choice, but in reality, mental formation already masterminded and prearranged everything for us in advance.

For example, we can talk about how mental formation already arranged for us to stay at the temple to listen to the Dharma teaching for only the morning session. We have come from very far away, and all of a sudden, we received a phone call after the morning teaching finished, and thus, we had to hurriedly rush home. We may think that this is a strange and unexpected occurrence that we ended up not being able to stay on to study in the afternoon, yet, mental formation already made pre-arrangement for it to happen.

Then, there are many happenings that seem quite normal which we think stem from our own choices, but there are other instances when we simply cannot choose. In the cases of those practitioners who have meditative absorption, however, can escape the pre-arrangement of the aggregate of mental formation. They can escape even if mental formation already masterminded everything so that each *karma* in our lives will happen in an orderly fashion from step one to step five, all the way to the very end. The force of the aggregate of mental formation is simply like that, and it is something which we cannot possibly break out nor flee from.

Since we are trapped in our bodies of five aggregates, the Buddha elucidated *"the five aggregates being Void"* in order to be emancipated from suffering. Otherwise, the aggregate of mental formation will continuously make arrangement for us life after life. We are completely stranded without a way out other than having to completely resolve the five aggregates. When we understand that we are being caught in the trap of mental formation just like this, if it still does not worry us, then no one would be able to unravel it for us. When we listen to the teaching up to this point, we realize that if we do not exert in our practice, the Historical Buddha, Mr. A or Mr. B cannot even rescue us. Even if there are a million Buddhas appearing in front of us, we would still not be able to break away from our bodies of five aggregates.

The Buddha clearly saw this, and thus, the only thing the Buddha did was to teach us how to practice and to provide us support for our practice. It is we, nevertheless, who must go beyond the five aggregates ourselves; otherwise, no one can stick their hands in to save us. Some doctrines say such and such a person can help us escape from this mundane world, but those are simply theories to mislead us. If we are being deluded in this life, our practice will be deadlocked. In this life, if we do not pour all of our energy into dismantling our five aggregates, then it seems that we would come out empty-handed. Because our progress would not continue to improve on its own in an orderly fashion. If and only if we can sustain and safeguard our practice exertion, then it is precisely this exertion power which can help us in our future lives.

For example, if we are currently still young, our practice may be quite weak, but as days go by, we will continue to be better, until one day, our practice will be far more superior superior than now. We can clearly see that following each year, our practice is definitely much improved and the power to control our *karmic* habitual tendencies is much stronger. Thus, when *karma* manifests, we can easily transform it. Our wisdom mind can penetratingly discern between right and wrong, good and bad, and at that time, we no longer are lured by the *karmic* force nor chase after attachment, anger and ignorance. If the power of our concentration absorption is stronger every moment until the very end, then it is precisely this force that will drive us forward in our consecutive future lives.

Due to the force of our practice, we will be able to advance in our next life. However, if we do not have any practice power, and mentally, there is neither change nor progress within us, then at the end of this life, the aggregate of mental formation will collect the old happenings for us to utilize in our next life. On the other hand, if we have meditative power, then we can implement this power, enough to prepare for our new life, and thus, in the next life, we will live with all the merits and wisdom which are the fruition of our prior practice. If we practice well until the end of life, then the aggregate of mental formation can also adjust and enhance our new life for the better. However, if we do not have any power from our practice, we do not recite the scriptures, are too lazy to sit in meditation, feel tormented and lamely cry when bad things happen, feel nostalgic, or are trapped in sadness and self-pity, then it means that there is no change in our mind as it remains normally mundane. If our mind is remains mundane, and we remain ordinary, then the aggregate of mental formation will arrange for us to follow our *karma.*

The aggregate of mental formation can pull out something from the past or some terrible incidents from billions and billions of lives ago back to the here and now. If our virtuous *karma* is powerful enough to overshadow the unwholesome *karma,* then the force of our practice exertion will gather all of our root virtues and wholesome *karmas* from infinite lifetimes into the new life so that we can utilize them them. In the approaching life, for example, if we accumulate ten virtues then we will enjoy the meritorious reward of ten virtues; additionally, our virtuous power would gather even more rewards from more wholesome deeds from the past. Thus, we would end up with a thousand meritorious rewards, and we will be able to live a truly wonderful life in the next life, we would at once meet the true spirituality at birth, and know how to practice in order to continue to progress in the cultivation of our practice efforts.

Our practice exertion will not go to waste, because it can maintain, preserve, and attract past virtuous deeds into the new life. If we can be in total control of *karma*, then the power of ignorance will not be strong enough when ignorance encounters mental formation. Because when the luminosity of our wisdom our meditative absorption suffice, then *karma* has no pulling force and we get to choose how to enter the embryo. Of course, we have *karma* with our [prospective] parents; however, if we see that this couple does not have enough merits to be our parents because their mind of virtues is not so great, whereas our virtuous mind is wholesome and we need to be in a different family, then we would search for another couple with a greater mind of virtues so that we can enter the embryo to become their child. Then, being a child of such a devoted family, they may bring us to the temple when we barely reach one or two years old, and that is the sole reason why we entered the embryo to become this couple's offspring. Therefore, if in this life we are not able to have self-control, then we would be perfectly helpless after we die. Once helpless, *karma* will whirl us away and we will have to accept the dominance of the aggregate of mental formation so that we would somehow be reborn in the new life.

Thus, aside from establishing our self-grasping, the aggregate of mental formation constructs all actions, gestures, words, actions and all other activities in this life which means our mental

59

formation nearly covers it all. For example, at the time being we are inspired and love to practice Zen, but the aggregate of mental formation already made arrangement so that in another ten years, we will end up following a Tantric master. At that time, we cannot possibly resist, and at the exact date and time, we will have all the ripened conditions to come across a master who is even more sublime than our master at the present with enough ability to lead us until the very end, and so, we will then follow in his footsteps.

We, therefore, cannot possibly determine anything for ourselves if we do not exert good practice. If we cultivate good practice, then we can decide on our own and make choices. If we do not cultivate good practice, then the aggregate of mental formation will arrange everything accordingly so that we can go on living step-by-step in this mundane world. We think that all of our resolutions and decisions are ours, just like how we think we are in control when we order foods. However, in reality, the way we did certain things on a certain day happens due to our *karmic* course of action. If we were more heedful, we would eat differently; if we were disturbed, we would eat differently. We would be able to recognize whether our mind is aware versus unalert during a meal. We can recognize either the influence of delusive desire, or our composed manner when ordering foods. These two mindsets and actions would come about very clearly. It is exactly the same for this life of ours. Everything is from the influencing power of the aggregate of mental formation, and it can construct everything and anything.

For people who have put an end to the aggregate of form, the aggregate of sensation and of perception so that they can all be Void, then the aggregate of mental formation is absolutely incredible; it can generate all the things that they ever want. Once the aggregate of perception is settled, all the things that originate from the aggregate of mental formation are actually the activation force in this life. If their mind are settled and calm, whatever they wish can take place accordingly although the five aggregates have not been extinguished. This is considered supramundane power. They can change everything in this life according to their desire if they want to. If they have the power to transcend the aggregate of perception, then they can do it, but they cannot if they have not yet gone beyond sense perception.

There is no measuring stick in this entire universe that can measure the depth, the breadth and the vigor of the aggregate of mental formation. Mental formation is the force of activation that gives birth to all phenomena. It is not yet our true *"innate nature,"* but it is connected to the vigorous force of the *"innate nature."* If the practitioner has transcended the aggregate of perception, settling deeply in meditative absorption for a long period, then he or she would see his or her body and mind as hollow void. They remain in *samadhi* or complete absorption, no longer disturbed, with their mind calm and pure and their mental suffering extinguished. The end of sense perception is the end of suffering, and many people think that *that* is already *Nirvāṇa* and thus, they abide in it until the end of their lives.

At the moment we exit this life, if we can transcend the aggregate of perception, then there will be a realm that is equivalent to the mind of those without perception. Living in such a realm, they continue to practice to dismantle the aggregate of mental formation and consciousness.

Truly, if we no longer carry a body, we would have a realm for those who have gone beyond perception; it is called the realm of non-perception. If we have wholesome conditions in this life, gathered together with our roots of virtues, virtuous *karma*, and our practice exertion from past lifetimes, then we may be able to transcend the aggregate of perception in this life. Even if we cannot yet cut through perception and simply suspend at the aggregate of perception, then this would have already been highly invaluable.

Of course, once we get here, we still need to advance further and not fall backward. After we enter deep meditative absorption, we will see an unending source, a living force that is overflowing from within our consciousness. In our mind, there is this current of life force that is so intense, yet it does not form anything. It operates very subtly and calmly, not emitting any waves of thoughts or thoughts itself. If we immerse in tranquility very profoundly so that our meditative absorption can be deeper and deeper, then we would be able to see from the outer veil all the way to the very depths of the aggregate of mental formation. The *karmic conscious seeds* will be penetratingly clear to us. The karmic seeds or the very *initial seeds of the life-and-death cycle* will be crystal clear and ever clearer to us – we directly see everything with clarity all the way down to the root of our cyclic origination.

However, before we can actually clearly see to the very depths of the root of life-and-death in the conscious aggregate, we must thoroughly penetrate and perfectly know all of the aggregate of mental formation from the outer to the inner core. The moment we become utterly immaculate, we would then be able to penetrate and directly see at that very instant *the very first initial vibrant motion of the aggregate of mental formation*. That is, actually, the very starting point of infinite lifetimes until now, which means we have now seen all the way back to the initial origination of the cycle of life-and-death, and therefore this cycle is considered fully resolved.

We must, after all, be able to immerse very deeply in complete absorption so that we can penetrate and directly see the very first *"primordial ripple"* in the aggregate of mental formation. This *"primordial ripple"* did not become a thought; it simply wiggled and led us to the path of life-and-death. It attracted infinite mental arising-and-ceasings – our thoughts – and let them overflow in our consciousness. When our wisdom is able to see the aggregate of mental formation all the way back to the very first initial starting point, then the cycle of life-and-death is considered fully resolved, and the aggregate of mental formation becomes extinct.

The aggregate of consciousness

The moment the aggregate of mental formation is extinct, we blaze as the splendor of clarity. Lucidity, pure radiance appears, but that is _not yet_ the perfect enlightenment, because we still see that there is a disparity between this luminous clarity and everything else around us. This luminosity is immaculate and all-pervading, yet it still sees a _"self"_ that is different from everything else. It illumines everything and recognizes everything surrounding it, although it is no longer a physical body. This is what is absolutely astonishing. This is, indeed, the aggregate of consciousness.

The aggregate of consciousness has the ability to know the past, the future, and each circumstance. It is all-knowing and all-discerning. Thus far, the meditative exertion experienced by many masters who came after the Buddha's time, and many of the existing meditation centers worldwide, seem unable to go beyond this stage and it is simply the aggregate of consciousness. Here, it is hollow and tranquil, boundlessly spacious, clearly knowing, and blazing with clarity. Here, it is extremely bright, yet, it cognizes that everything else is _not_ itself. There is still a _"knowing-awareness"_ that is pure, hollow and tranquil, boundlessly vast, all-pervasive. There is nothing that it does not know, yet, it does not generate any discriminating, dualistic thoughts, and there is no comparison whatsoever in this state of being. This is a quiet, subtle cognition and knowingness – a quiet, subtle awareness that is extremely minuscule and so deep within us – and at that moment, we see that we are truly very tranquil. Nevertheless, there still exists this *"self"* – a "self" of ours that is tranquil. The tranquility is still this *"self"* of ours; the void is still this *"self"* of ours; thus, we have not yet *exhausted the selves!* So we must understand that this is simply the tranquil sphere of the aggregate of consciousness, not enlightenment, because there is still this *"self"* of ours who knows. This silent ever-knowingness exists similarly to our *"innate nature" (our True Nature)* however, the ultimate knowingness of our *"innate nature"* is different.

Right now and right here, at this stage, it may very well be that we can see it all, hear it all, and our six-sense faculties in the vivid presence know it all. The eye consciousness, ear consciousness, nose consciousness, tongue consciousness, body consciousness and mental consciousness exist lucidly within the six-sense organs and they clearly know all phenomena, but they do not give rise to any dualistic thinking. Still, they see themselves different from the other phenomena, as they themselves are not one with form, sound, smell, taste, touch or objects of mind. They simply know form, sound, smell, taste, touch and objects of mind. They clearly cognize without having any discrimination, yet, they *are still not yet* form, sound, smell, taste, touch or objects of mind.

The practitioner, therefore, needs to know that he is still being trapped in discriminating consciousness. At that moment, although it is a clear knowingness, the sense of *"distinctiveness"* has not been utterly extinguished—there is still a discrete quietude, a distinguished sense of singularity that still lingers on. Therefore, even though we can be illumined and crystal clear, if there is still a *"self"* somewhere to be illumined, then as practitioners, we must recognize this fault. If we do not see this fault, then we have not yet emancipated. Here is actually the talisman on the top of the Wu Tai Shan Mountain, and here is where the monkey of consciousness needs to stir up all the way to reach the *Ālaya* consciousness. The *Ālaya* consciousness will see that there is <u>still</u> something here that needs to be extricated. To extricate the dissimilarity between this *"self"* and all *"phenomena"* means, in that very instant, we – our so-called *"selves"* – dissolve and actually become one with the entire *dharmdhātu*, the realm of truth. There is no longer self versus phenomena. Once the dissimilarity is removed, the *"self"* utterly disappears, and what is left is the lucid noumenal state.

Therefore, we must see such a fault when we ourselves are still being different from *"something else."* This is actually the last fault of our discriminating consciousness! At this stage, we have *"knowing,"* but there is still *"this self who knows."* If so, then *"this self who knows"* must also dissipate. Once we reach there, the power of activation will automatically push us through, because if we have already gone beyond the aggregate of mental formation, it would be quite easy for us to pull through during this practice segment. Well, it may be easy to say so, but one still needs some time to practice meticulously; one cannot be vague about this, because if one becomes laid-back, and cannot maintain or nourish one's practice during this critical segment, then one cannot possibly disintegrate the *"silent, subtle self."* Once one reaches here, one really needs to diligently maintain and nourish one's practice!

Thus, in regards to this silent, subtle knowing awareness, we need a discrete place for ourselves to practice so that we can settle deeply in this quietude of knowingness. This *"quiet, subtle knowing-awareness"* is still being distinct from all *dharmas.* Therefore, it means that if we are still being slightly differentiated from a grain of sand, a breeze, a light, or slightly dissimilar from something else, then that means there is still the duality of *"self"* and *"phenomena."*

66

It means that, at this stage, there is still a *"self,"* and we must, by all means, recognize this fault! It is because if there were still a *"self"* over here, then there would be a *"him/her/it"* over there. However, the very moment we finally recognize and have a direct knowing that there is a *"self"* still *"existing within this knowing-awareness,"* then at that very instant the *"self"* will dissipate. We, or the *"self,"* will spontaneously disappear. We are now *"not two."* We are now" *non-dual"* from the flowers, the leaves, the empty space, the universe, and the all-pervasiveness itself. At that moment, our outmoded *"self"* is automatically exhausted.

Yet, when we arrive at this point in our practice, there will be another *"death,"* the death of all of the differentiations and discriminations, so that *the very vivid presence* will have neither more differentiation nor discrimination, and there will no longer be any dissimilarity among all phenomena that are *"clearly emerging"* in this vivid presence. Right then it will simply be the *"equanimous, non-discriminative presence,"* and this is crossing of the last threshold of the aggregate of consciousness!

This is not at all an easy thing to reach here, yet, when talking about transcending the five aggregates, many practitioners mistakenly perceive that they have attained ultimate realization. If there is an exceptional teacher and he can see through us, then it would be easy for us when we reach this point in our practice. Most of the Zen masters would wait for their disciples to reach this point so that the masters can *"knock-on"* them. If the disciples have only dismantled the aggregate of perception, then it may not be possible for the masters to knock-on them, but once they have reached this point, then yes, it is possible. Those practitioners who transcend perception can be sitting right there, yet, the gods cannot even find them to make an offering to them even if the gods want to.

Even so, it means the practitioners have only dismantled perception, not yet reaching the last threshold of consciousness. Thus, if a master with vigorous power wants to whack his student so that he or she can pass through the aggregate of mental formation, or be emancipated from the aggregate of consciousness to at least once immerse in the *"five aggregates being Void,"* then it is not at all easy! Such a practitioner needs assistance in his practice exertion; he himself needs to maintain and nourish his practice, and he himself needs to realize that he has not yet reached the final destination.

The extinction of perception can lead people to have supramundane power, but to have this kind of power before reaching full attainment can easily make one err on the path. It would be quite easy to give rise to a mind of self-proclamation, believing that one has attained sainthood or *Arhatship*. If so, it can be considered the "end of life," because one still has not yet dismantled the rest that follows. These practitioners will not return to take rebirth as human beings, but they will exist in their own realms. In this kind of realms, they will continue to abide in such a state of emptiness for a very long time before they can emancipate from this state. The Buddhas and Bodhisattvas would have to go there to give pith instructions to them so that they can actually depart from these perpetual realms; otherwise, these practitioners will forever grasp the quiescent, serene, pure, and ecstatic state of being even though they still have *two more layers to transcend* before the cycle of life-and-death can be exhausted. The extinction of the aggregate of perception does not mean that one can attain the final transmundane power of the utter extinguishment of all mental defilements; one has to completely dismantle *both aggregates of mental formation and consciousness* before one can attain this transmundane power.

We can see that talking about the aggregate of consciousness can be never-ending. However, once the practitioner recognizes the primordial origin, the initial beginning, or the sprouting source since beginningless time, and once the *"subtle vibrant motion"* in the aggregate of mental formation that *initially* led him to the cycle of life-and-death is resolved, then right at that moment he can leap over the aggregate of consciousness and completely dissolve!

When life-and-death is utterly dissipated, one can transcend the three worlds, and usually it is just like that. This pair of *"mental formation–consciousness"* will disappear altogether at the same time. Because the practitioner had cultivated meditation absorption for a very, very long time, so this decisive moment is similar to what is mentioned in the practice of extinguishing the ten fetters, during which the practitioner already transcends restlessness which is the covert lair of mental formation, yet there is still the *"subtle vital faculty"* or *"vital base"* which is the life continuum. This subtle vital self, the self-grasping, the illusionary self and the thought-based self still exists within the boundless, empty realm of peace and serenity.

Yet, the instant the *supreme sacred wisdom beyond mind* of an awakened being appears, ignorance is utterly dispelled. When benighted ignorance is extinguished, we get to see the innermost truth. When this truth reveals itself, we will be able to penetrate our self-grasping, and when self-grasping dissolves, the vital faculty or vital base comes to an end, and only when ignorance is completely purified, then we can attain sainthood. Actually, the *"very last pinpoint of subtle self-grasping"* is precisely this consciousness! Therefore, when we can annihilate birth and death in the aggregate of mental formation, we would have enough radiant clarity to see that the subtle self-grasping is indeed the aggregate of consciousness. It is diminutive, quietly subdued, silently calm, and it *"exists,"* yet, is utterly *"non-existent."* However, this is not yet the Abiding Sphere of Neither Perception nor Non-Perception (the Eighth Meditative Absorption State).

At this stage, consciousness is different from the Abiding Sphere of Neither Perception nor Non-Perception. Although this consciousness is silently subtle, it no longer has sensation or form. This consciousness is no longer perception, feelings nor volition. This consciousness is the tranquil knowing-awareness and the very last covert lair. Although it is something so diminutive, it is the ending one! If we can dismantle this ending point, and see all the way to the initial vibrant sprout – the very root source of our mental formation – that which leads us to the endless cycle of life-and-death, then the aggregate of mental formation would automatically dissipate. At that very moment, we will blaze in radiant clarity and can *go beyond the aggregate of consciousness.* There will simply be the perfect and complete existence of the expanse of phenomenal truth in the presence without any dissimilarity whatsoever, which means we finally transcend the aggregate of consciousness.

In reality, we do not arrive here due to our exertion in practice, but because our vigor has become our *"internal driving force"* following the extinction of the aggregate of perception. Once perception is distinguished, our inner force will be immense, and only then can it submerge deeply in the aggregate of mental formation and dismantle the aggregate of consciousness. However, the initial gate leading to awakening is still the aggregate of form. If anyone who receives the pith instructions from a spiritual master without having to exert in practice to dismantle the form aggregate, then in their own life, he or she would have to come back to living through days and months with the *"form aggregate as being Void."* They would still be completely living as they actually witness how each of the physical cells goes through their own *"death"*— which means the practitioner actually goes through the experience and realization of *"strolling the synthesis of form as Void, sensation as Void, perception as Void, mental formation as Void, and consciousness as Void."* Thereafter, this practitioner can finally be utterly unobstructed. Otherwise, if the practitioner has not yet passed through this experience, then they cannot be unimpeded. They may be able to realize it theoretically, but it is not yet fully unobstructed. Only by reaching this final stage that it can be called the *"five aggregates being Void."*

ABOUT ZEN MASTER THÍCH TUỆ HẢI

Senior Venerable Zen Master Thích Tuệ Hải whose Dharma name means *"Ocean of Wisdom"* (birth name: Đinh Kim Nga, also known as *Vô Trụ Thiền Sư* or *Hiển Hiện Như Nhiên Thiền Sư)* was born in 1968 in Long Thới Village, Chợ Lách District, Bến Tre Pro-vince. Master Tuệ Hải came from a land-owner family and was the youngest of seven children. The land on which he was born was thought to be sacred, because during the war, bombings and gunfire never reached it. Thus, many people in nearby areas would escape to his family's land in search of sanctuary.

One day, following an upheaval Master Tuệ Hải's father gave up his career, and his family found themselves in very difficult circumstances. As two of his older brothers took to heart the meaning of impermanence, they decided to become *bhikkhus*. Thereafter, his older sister also became a *bhikkuni*.

Since his childhood, Master Tuệ Hải has been very filial toward his parents. At the age of six, he already knew how to cook a meal, and in order to support his family, he would follow his mother to help her sell things at the market. At night, he would come back home to take care of his father with much love and devotion, always serving and following his father's wishes without even the slightest thought of objection. Tuệ Hải said, "I was raised over very difficult circumstances ever since I was a young child; therefore, I was equipped with a strong determination to overcome arduous, challenging life situations until this very day."

His mother, on the other hand, was a peaceful, wondrous woman who was full of loving-kindness and free from discord. Master Tuệ Hải used to say: "It would be difficult to find another woman throughout this world with as wonderful qualities as my mother." His mother spent her entire life devoting to her family, and in 1993, she became an ordained nun, learning and practicing the Dharma at Tuệ Không Monastery.

Accompanied by great roots of virtues planted in the Buddha-Dharma, Master Tuệ Hải, at the age of seven, became deeply moved the very first time he saw the statue of Buddha Shakyamuni. He stood immobile and entered meditative absorption in front of the statue for close to eight hours during which he was completely aware of everything that took place around him. Many people witnessed this and they did not dare to disturb Master Tuệ Hải until he left the meditative state himself.

In 1985, Zen Master Thích Tuệ Hải fell severely ill and began to research and study the macrobiotic diet method of Sir G. Oshawa. He followed the nutritional macrobiotic diet for just twenty-one days and reached the so-called Diet #7 empirical experience. It was the state of perfect complimentary yin-yang balance just as Sir G. Oshawa had indicated. All illnesses, therefore, disappeared, and throughout those seven days and nights, Master Tuệ Hải remained in a tranquil state of emptiness of body and mind with boundless bliss and happiness.

In that very same year, while still a young student, Master Tuệ Hải was listening to his teacher give a lecture on the subject of *"All things are set in motion in space"* during which he suddenly realized the principle of impermanence, and therefore, began to build the determination to become ordained. It was not until the beginning of 1986 that Tuệ Hải left his household for Thường Chiếu Zen Monastery where he would begin his volunteer work and Dharma studies to prepare for his ordination.

On December 8, 1986, which fell on the anniversary of the Buddha's Great Enlightenment, Master Tuệ Hải officially received ordination from the Grand Master Thích Thanh Từ and was given the Dharma name Tuệ Hải *(Ocean of Wisdom)*. When living with the other monks in the monastery, he was assigned to toil the land and to grow vegetables; however, his aspiration to gain liberation from the mundane world, to resolutely transcend life-and-death and to merge with the absolute truth, continued to be his burning desire. As months and years passed by, the yearning in his heart grew more intensively, until one day, on July 7, 1997, as he listened to his Root Teacher, the Great Master Thích Thanh Từ, explain Nāgārjuna's Middle Way (*Mādhyamika-Shastra*), he heard the following comment, *"the emptiness of sensation is Nirvāṇa,"* and at that very moment, immediately severed all kinds of past and present conventional knowledge. With his mind and body empty and clear, he thoroughly and lucidly realized that all conditions and object-appearances were no longer the same physical form aggregate as he had always known.

Since then, Master Tuệ Hải fathomed the sublime teachings and no longer had any doubts regarding the words of the Buddha; he has fully comprehended the perfect truth, and from an understanding that transcends all conventions, life has become nonchalant and leisurely calm. At that very moment, he appreciatively composed a verse depicting this living force within him:

> From now on, to leisurely live in happiness,
> Each condition brightly lucid and non-mistaken
> Non-mistaken, unconfused, unerring,
> Simply radiant, just like that – how is it possible to express it fully!

On December 12, 1994, Master Thích Tuệ Hải followed the command of his Root Teacher, the Grand Master Thích Thanh Từ, who appointed him to become the Abbot of Long Hương Temple in Nhơn Trạch District, Đồng Nai Province, where he presently resides. Zen Master Thích Tuệ Hải has taught extensively on Mahāyāna Zen, the true nature of the mind, and on various major *Sūtras,* especially the *Avataṃsaka* Sūtra *(Flower Ornament Sūtra)* and its vast and profound view, similar to the pure view of Vajrayana that all *dharmas* are equanimous, non-discriminatory, and are actually Buddhas. In all of his teachings, Master Tuệ Hải always tries to point out the singleness and true essence of all traditions, whether it is Theravāda, Mahāyāna, Pureland, Zen or Vajrayana. His greatest aspiration is for all the diverse traditions of Buddhism to have a unified view in accordance with the realized and liberated view as taught by Buddha: *"Hundreds of rivers together flow to the vast sea; as the sea has a single salty taste, my Dharma, too, has only a single taste of liberation."*

Aside from propagating the Dharma to benefit beings, Master Tuệ Hải is also a physician of traditional medicine and macrobiotics who has cured many severe illnesses, and has advised everyone to develop a healthy balance of body and mind in order to unlock one's inner wisdom, to understand the natural order of the universe, and to gain limitless freedom, absolute impartiality, and endless bliss and happiness.

In 2009 and 2012, Zen Master Tuệ Hải traveled extensively and taught in over forty states in the USA, as well as Europe and Australia. Thereafter, he chose to remain in Vietnam to oversee the long-term construction of the new Long Hương Temple, as well as to provide weekly teachings and spiritual guidance to local Buddhist communities and the newly established ordained sangha at his Temple. Currently, Zen Master Thích Tuệ Hải remains a Senior Standing Committee Member of the Educational Committee of the Central Buddhist Congregation in Vietnam.

Gone

Gone

Gone Beyond

Gone Utterly Freely Beyond

Perfectly Awakened

Svāhā

Essence of Prajñāpāramitā

Printed in Great Britain
by Amazon

39100917R00045